BEST COBBLERS & CRISPS EVER

BEST COBBLERS & CRISPS EVER

NO-FAIL RECIPES FOR RUSTIC FRUIT DESSERTS

MONICA SWEENEY

THE COUNTRYMAN PRESS

A DIVISION OF W. W. NORTON & COMPANY

INDEPENDENT PUBLISHERS SINCE 1923

All photographs by Allan Penn, unless otherwise noted below:

Page 10, 11: © sematadesign/Shutterstock.com; 13: © Olha_Afanasieva/iStockphoto.com; 15: © Anna Hoychuk/Shutterstock.com; 17, 25: © cobraphotography/Shutterstock.com; 19, 23: © vm2002/Shutterstock.com; 21: © Unknown/Shutterstock.com; 27: © msheldrake/iStockphoto.com; 29: © YuliaKotina/Shutterstock.com; 31, 61: © Mshev/Shutterstock.com; 33: © Yulia_Kotina/iStockphoto.com; 35: © manyakotic/iStockphoto.com; 37, 65: © Anna_Pustynnikova/Shutterstock.com; 38, 39, 53: © Ildi Papp/Shutterstock.com; 41: © kitty/Shutterstock.com; 43: © kourafas5/iStockphoto.com; 45: © AnjelikaGr/Shutterstock.com; 47: © Elena Shashkina/Shutterstock.com; 49: © manyakotic/iStockphoto.com; 51: © Tatiana Volgutova/Shutterstock.com; 55, 73: © Brent Hofacker/Shutterstock.com; 57: bhofack2/iStockphoto.com; 59: © StephanieFrey/iStockphoto.com; 62, 63: © Shebeko/Shutterstock.com; 67: © sarsmis/Shutterstock.com; 69: © loooby/iStockphoto.com; 71: © Tanya_F/iStockphoto.com; 75: © Elena Demyanko/Shutterstock.com; 77: © Sea Wave/Shutterstock.com; 79: © Vladislav Nosik/Shutterstock.com; 81: © Liliya Kandrashevich/Shutterstock.com; 83: © vikif/iStockphoto.com; 85: © Dar1930/iStockphoto.com; 86, 87: © Maria Komar/Shutterstock.com; 89: © Kemih/Shutterstock.com; 91: © Melissandra/iStockphoto.com; 95: © Amallia Eka/Shutterstock.com; 97: © Anna Shepulova/Shutterstock.com; 99: © Nataliya Arzamasova/Shutterstock.com; 105: © Ulyana Khorunzha/Shutterstock.com; 108, 109: © MaraZe/Shutterstock.com

For information about permission to reproduce selections from this book, write to Permissions, The Countryman Press, 500 Fifth Avenue, New York, NY 10110

For information about special discounts for bulk purchases, please contact W. W. Norton Special Sales at specialsales@wwnorton.com or 800-233-4830.

Library of Congress Cataloging-in-Publication Data
Names: Sweeney, Monica, author.
Title: Best cobblers & crisps ever : no-fail recipes for rustic fruit desserts / Monica Sweeney.
Other titles: Best cobblers and crisps ever
Description: Woodstock, VT : Countryman Press, a division of W. W. Norton & Company, Independent Publishers Since 1923, [2016] |
Includes bibliographical references and index.
Identifiers: LCCN 2015045181 | ISBN 9781581573923 (pbk. : alk. paper)
Subjects: LCSH: Cobblers (Cooking) | LCGFT: Cookbooks.
Classification: LCC TX773 .S9864 2016 | DDC 641.86/52—dc23
LC record available at http://lccn.loc.gov/2015045181

The Countryman Press
www.countrymanpress.com

A division of W. W. Norton & Company, Inc.,
500 Fifth Avenue, New York, NY 10110
www.wwnorton.com

10 9 8 7 6 5 4 3 2 1

TO AIMEE CHASE,
FOR YOUR TWO CENTS AND MORE.

BEST COBBLERS & CRISPS EVER
CONTENTS

Introduction

Some of the very best foods are the simplest ones. All it can take is a bit of piping hot fruit with a crispy topping, pulled fresh from the oven, to transport you somewhere special. These no-frills desserts are classics for two reasons: they are easy to prepare, and they rely on the natural, delectable flavors of fresh fruit to carry their weight.

These fruity delights go by a variety of names—everything from cobblers, crisps, and crumbles to grunts, slumps, betties, and buckles. Generally speaking, a crisp is a baked fruit dish with oats atop it, and crumbles are topped with flavored breadcrumbs. Cobblers are a bit distinct, as they generally feature biscuit dough that has been dropped by the spoonful onto the fruit filling, creating what looks like cobblestones (hence the name). Betties are sometimes just another version of a crisp—topped with buttery, sugary streusel, with or without oats. Grunts and slumps are skillet-cooked cobblers, and buckles tend to have cakey batter underneath the fruit, rather than atop it. Whatever you call them in your house, there's no denying that these incredible blends of sweet fruit and savory toppings taste like home.

When making these recipes, keep in mind that the cooking pan you choose will not make or break your dessert. Most of the recipes call for an 8-inch baking dish or ramekin, but you can use what you have available. The delights of cobblers, crisps, and crumbles may traditionally start with apples or peaches—but to stop there would practically be a culinary crime. The endless possible combinations of fruits, flavors, textures, and spices can turn a seemingly unremarkable traditional dessert into something truly delectable. Each chapter of this book highlights different fruits; we start with berries, stone fruit, and orchard fruit, and move on to the tropical and the autumnal varieties.

Ultimately, if you take away anything from this book, it should be that the recipes for these treats are incredibly forgiving. Don't have enough oats to top your crisp? Toss in some nuts to add an extra crunch. Tired of the heaven-sent buttery, flaky cobbler biscuits? (Hey, anything is possible.) Try adding some extra flavors like cocoa powder, vanilla, or ginger to the batter. We've also included some recipes for great tasting whipped creams and sauces to dollop or drizzle over any of these flavor-packed, oven-baked treats. The opportunities are endless—and this assortment of dessert options is only the beginning.

CHAPTER ONE

BLUEBERRIES, STRAWBERRIES, RASPBERRIES, AND MORE

Raspberry Shortbread Cookie Crumble

Buttery shortbread, sweet and tart raspberries, and a hint of coconut—this crumble is both comforting and nuanced. The cooked raspberries will be piping hot and melt decadently into the shortbread. When plating the dessert, toss some fresh, chilled raspberries on top for garnish.

Yield: 6–8 servings

FILLING

4 cups raspberries

¼ cup sugar

¼ cup all-purpose flour

¼ teaspoon cinnamon

SHORTBREAD TOPPING

½ cup (1 stick) unsalted butter

¾ cup granulated sugar

¼ teaspoon kosher salt

1 teaspoons vanilla extract

1 egg yolk

1 cup all-purpose flour

½ cup sweetened shredded coconut, toasted

Filling
Preheat the oven to 350°F. Grease an 8-inch baking dish. In the baking dish, gently toss the berries with the sugar, flour, and cinnamon until the berries are coated evenly.

Topping
In a separate bowl, combine the butter, sugar, salt, and vanilla until smooth. Mix in the egg. Gradually add in the flour and mix until combined. Fold in the coconut. Crumble the shortbread dough evenly over the top of the filling. Bake for 25 minutes or until the crumble is golden brown and the juices are bubbling.

Blueberry Crisp

This no-frills crisp lets blueberries stand alone for a reason. When you've already got the flavors of crunchy, crispy oats, brown sugar, and cinnamon, the classic tartness of oven-hot blueberries is all you really need. Serve with a scoop of vanilla ice cream or with a dollop of fresh whipped cream for a truly homey indulgence.

Yield: 6–8 servings

FILLING

4 cups blueberries

¼ cup sugar

¼ cup all-purpose flour

¼ teaspoon cinnamon

TOPPING

¾ cup all-purpose flour

½ cup brown sugar

2 tablespoons granulated sugar

¼ teaspoon nutmeg

½ teaspoon kosher salt

½ cup (1 stick) unsalted butter

1 cup old-fashioned oats

Filling

Preheat the oven to 350°F. Grease an 8-inch baking dish or ramekin. In the baking dish, gently toss the berries with the sugar, flour, and cinnamon until the fruit is coated evenly.

Topping

In a separate bowl, combine the flour, sugars, nutmeg, and salt. Slice the butter into pats and add to the mixture. Mix the butter and the dry ingredients, except the oats, until blended. Add the oats and knead the mixture until it becomes clumpy. Sprinkle the topping evenly over the filling. Bake for 30 to 40 minutes or until the top is golden brown and the juices are bubbling.

Tri-Berry Crumble

Whether you went all-in at the farmer's market or you just happen to have a bag of mixed berries in your freezer, this triad of sweetness is the perfect fit for a delicious berry crisp. If you are working with frozen berries, let them defrost before baking and reduce the cooking time by about 10 minutes.

Yield: 6–8 servings

FILLING

2 cups blackberries

1 cup blueberries

1 cup raspberries

½ cup sugar

¼ cup all-purpose flour

¼ teaspoon cinnamon

TOPPING

¾ cup all-purpose flour

½ cup brown sugar

2 tablespoons granulated sugar

¼ teaspoon nutmeg

½ teaspoon kosher salt

½ cup (1 stick) unsalted butter

1 cup old-fashioned oats

Filling

Preheat the oven to 350°F. Grease an 8-inch baking dish. In the baking dish, gently toss the berries with the sugar, flour, and cinnamon until the fruit is coated evenly.

Topping

In a separate bowl, combine the flour, sugars, nutmeg, and salt. Slice the butter into pats and add to the mixture. Mix the butter and the dry ingredients except the oats until blended. Add the oats and knead the mixture until it becomes clumpy. Sprinkle the topping evenly over the filling. Bake for 30 to 40 minutes or until the top is golden brown and the juices are bubbling.

Pear-Blueberry Crisp

A surprising mix of texture and tartness, this pear and blueberry combination is a pleasant detour from a traditional blueberry crisp. If you are baking and serving the crisp in ramekins rather than in a larger dish, make sure to slice the pears into smaller chunks so that there is a nice balance of the two fruits. The addition of almonds offers an added crunch to the traditional crisp topping, making this a warming dessert that is full of sweet surprises.

Yield: 6–8 servings

FILLING

2 cups chopped pears (about 2 large)

2 cups blueberries

¼ cup granulated sugar

¼ cup all-purpose flour

¼ teaspoon cinnamon

TOPPING

¾ cup all-purpose flour

½ cup brown sugar

2 tablespoons granulated sugar

¼ teaspoon nutmeg

½ teaspoon kosher salt

½ cup (1 stick) unsalted butter

¾ cup old-fashioned oats

¼ cup sliced almonds, toasted

Filling

Preheat the oven to 350°F. Grease an 8 inch baking dish. In the baking dish, gently toss the pears and blueberries with the sugar, flour, and cinnamon until the fruit is coated evenly.

Topping

In a separate bowl, combine the flour, sugars, nutmeg, and salt. Slice the butter into pats and add to the mixture. Mix the butter and the dry ingredients except the oats until blended. Add the oats and almonds, kneading the mixture until it becomes clumpy. Sprinkle the topping evenly over the filling. Bake for 40 to 50 minutes or until the top is golden brown and the juices are bubbling.

Strawberry-Rhubarb Cobbler with Mint

Rhubarb has no greater calling than flavoring a steaming hot seasonal cobbler. Depending on where you live, this stalky plant might be classified as a veggie rather than a fruit. But whichever way you spin it, rhubarb shines when baked in this delightful mix of strawberry and mint. The toasty cobbler biscuits are part flaky goodness, part sponge to the flavors of this lovely dessert.

Yield: 6–8 servings

FILLING

2 cups rhubarb, sliced crosswise

3 cups strawberries, hulled and quartered

½ cup granulated sugar

2 tablespoons fresh lime juice

¼ cup all-purpose flour

TOPPING

1½ cups all-purpose flour

¼ cup granulated sugar

1½ teaspoons baking powder

¼ teaspoon kosher salt

1 teaspoon lime zest

1½ tablespoons unsalted butter, chilled

1 cup buttermilk

Sprigs of fresh mint for garnish

Filling

Preheat the oven to 350°F. Grease an 8 inch baking dish. In a saucepan, combine the rhubarb, 1½ cups strawberries, granulated sugar, and lime juice until the fruit is coated evenly. On medium-low heat, cook the mixture until the sugar dissolves and the fruit begins to juice, about 3 minutes. Bring to a boil, and then add the flour until the fruit thickens after 2 minutes or so. Take the fruit off the heat, add the remaining strawberries and mint, and transfer to the baking dish.

Topping

In a separate bowl, combine the flour, granulated sugar, baking powder, salt, and lime zest. Slice the butter into pats and cut into the flour mixture with a pastry cutter or fork until crumbly. Add the buttermilk and fold into the dry ingredients until just combined. Drop the dough by rounded tablespoons onto the filling. Bake for 25 to 30 minutes or until the top is golden brown and the juices are bubbling. Garnish with fresh sprigs of mint.

Skillet Blueberry-Basil Cobbler

There are few better pairings than blueberries and basil. The homey flavor of a warm blueberry cobbler is good enough on its own, but the kick of basil adds an extra bit of excitement to this fantastic dessert.

Yield: 6–8

FILLING

2 cups blueberries

¼ cup basil, finely chopped

1 tablespoon granulated sugar

TOPPING

1 cup all-purpose flour

1 cup granulated sugar

1 teaspoon baking powder

½ teaspoon kosher salt

1 teaspoon lemon zest

1 cup milk

2 tablespoons fresh lemon juice

1 teaspoon vanilla

Sprigs of fresh basil or mint for garnish

Filling

Preheat the oven to 350°F. Heavily grease a 10-inch cast-iron skillet and let it warm in the oven. Gently toss the blueberries, basil, and sugar together and set them aside.

Topping

In a separate bowl, combine the flour, sugar, baking powder, salt, and lemon zest. Whisk in the milk, lemon juice, and vanilla until combined. Carefully remove the skillet from the oven and add the blueberry mixture. Pour the batter over the blueberry mixture. Return the skillet to the oven and bake for 30 minutes or until the top is golden brown and the juices are bubbling. Garnish with fresh basil or mint.

Huckleberry Cobbler

Huckleberries, the blueberry's sweeter cousin, have a special place in my heart. In the Northeast, they aren't always available, but a friend of mine from Idaho introduced me to huckleberry teas and jams. I always try and take advantage of these when I come across them, and a cobbler is a delightful way to make use of them. Top this one with a bit of homemade whipped cream for a nice way to bring out the huckleberry.

Yield: 6–8 servings

FILLING

4 cups huckleberries

½ cup sugar

1 tablespoon cornstarch

1 tablespoon fresh lemon juice

TOPPING

1½ cups all-purpose flour

¼ cup granulated sugar

1½ teaspoons baking powder

¼ teaspoon baking soda

¼ teaspoon kosher salt

1 teaspoon lemon zest

1½ tablespoons unsalted butter, melted

¾ cup buttermilk

Filling

Preheat the oven to 400°F. Grease an 8-inch baking dish or ramekins. In the baking dish or a bowl, gently toss the huckleberries with the sugar, cornstarch, and lemon juice until the berries are coated evenly. Transfer mixture to ramekins, if applicable.

Topping

In a separate bowl, combine the flour, granulated sugar, baking powder, baking soda, salt, and lemon zest. Add the butter and the buttermilk and fold into the dry ingredients until just combined. Drop the dough by rounded tablespoons onto the filling. Bake for 30 to 40 minutes or until the top is golden brown and the juices are bubbling.

Strawberry Cobbler

A sweet strawberry cobbler is great for an afternoon picnic on a breezy summer day. Even if the seasons and weather aren't in your favor, this is a simple, easygoing dessert that's just as easy to whip up with frozen strawberries.

Yield: 6–8 servings

FILLING

4 cups strawberries

½ cup sugar

1 tablespoon cornstarch

1 tablespoon fresh lemon juice

TOPPING

1½ cups all-purpose flour

¼ cup granulated sugar

1½ teaspoons baking powder

¼ teaspoon baking soda

¼ teaspoon kosher salt

1 teaspoon lemon zest

1½ tablespoons unsalted butter, melted

¾ cup buttermilk

Filling

Preheat the oven to 400°F. Grease an 8-inch baking dish. In the baking dish or a bowl, gently toss the strawberries with the sugar, cornstarch, and lemon juice until the berries are coated evenly.

Topping

In a separate bowl, combine the flour, granulated sugar, baking powder, baking soda, salt, and lemon zest. Add the butter and the buttermilk and fold into the dry ingredients until just combined. Drop the dough by rounded tablespoons onto the filling. Bake for 30 to 40 minutes or until the top is golden brown and the juices are bubbling.

Red Currant Cobbler Bars

Red currants! These berries don't get nearly enough love. They have the bursting juices of a fresh pomegranate—but without the seedy, clothes-staining aftereffects. I've used freshly picked red currants in popovers and pancakes to great success, but these bars are an even better treat. If you like the taste of licorice, try using black currants.

Yield: 24 small bars

CRUST

1 cup granulated sugar

3 cups all-purpose flour

1 teaspoon baking powder

¼ teaspoon salt

1 teaspoon lemon zest

1 cup (2 sticks) unsalted butter, chilled

1 egg

FILLING

½ cup white sugar

4 teaspoons cornstarch

2 tablespoons fresh lemon juice

4 cups fresh red currants

Crust

Preheat the oven to 375°F. Grease a 9 x 13-inch baking dish. Combine the sugar, flour, baking powder, salt, and lemon zest. Add the butter and the egg until the dough is crumbly. Separate the mixture into two equal parts, and press one portion of the dough to the bottom of the baking dish.

Filling

In a separate bowl, combine the sugar, cornstarch, and lemon juice. Fold in the currants until combined evenly. Spread the currant mixture evenly across the first layer of dough. Crumble the remaining dough over the fruit. Bake for 30 to 40 minutes or until the crumble is golden brown. Allow to cool before cutting.

Blueberry-Coconut Crumble Bars

A blueberry dessert with a bit of a tropical twist, these crumble bars get all the best parts of a blueberry crumble with the added perks of flaky coconut. If you're a macaroon lover (or just a chocolate lover), add a half-cup of chocolate chips to the crust for an even more indulgent treat.

Yield: 24 small bars

CRUST

1 cup granulated sugar

3 cups all-purpose flour

1 teaspoon baking powder

¼ teaspoon salt

1 teaspoon lemon zest

1 cup (2 sticks) unsalted butter, chilled

1 egg

FILLING

½ cup granulated sugar

4 teaspoons cornstarch

1 cup shredded coconut

2 tablespoons lemon juice

4 cups fresh blueberries

Crust

Preheat the oven to 375°F. Grease a 9 x 13-inch baking dish. Combine the sugar, flour, baking powder, salt, and lemon zest. Add the butter and the egg until the dough is crumbly. Separate the mixture in half, pressing half the dough to the bottom of the baking dish.

Filling

In a separate bowl, combine the sugar, cornstarch, coconut, and lemon juice. Fold in the blueberries until combined evenly. Spread the blueberry mixture evenly across the first layer of dough. Crumble the remaining dough over the fruit. Bake for 30 to 40 minutes or until the crumble is golden brown. Allow to cool before cutting.

Blueberry-Butterscotch Betty Bars

There is no finer dessert than an alliterative one. The salty-sweetness of butter-scotch makes these blueberry betty bars something to be savored. Just be careful not to eat all the chips before you've had a chance to add them to the recipe! Enjoy these buttery and delicious, crumbly confections any time of day.

Yield: 24 small bars

CRUST

1 cup granulated sugar

3 cups all-purpose flour

1 teaspoon baking powder

¼ teaspoon salt

1 cup (2 sticks) unsalted butter, chilled

1 egg

½ cup butterscotch chips

FILLING

½ cup granulated sugar

4 teaspoons cornstarch

4 cups fresh blueberries

Crust

Preheat the oven to 375°F. Grease a 9 x 13-inch baking dish. Combine the sugar, flour, baking powder, and salt. Add the butter and the egg until the dough is crumbly. Fold in the butterscotch chips. Separate the mixture in half, pressing half the dough to the bottom of the baking dish.

Filling

In a separate bowl, combine the sugar and cornstarch. Fold in the blueberries until combined evenly. Spread the blueberry mixture evenly across the first layer of dough. Crumble the remaining dough over the fruit. Bake for 30 to 40 minutes or until the crumble is golden brown. Allow to cool before cutting.

White-Chocolate Raspberry Crisp Bars

These wonderful bars have the tartness of raspberries, the zesty citrus of orange, the smoothness of white chocolate, and the satisfying crunch of crispy oats. The white chocolate chips add all sorts of extra goodness, but if you're not a white chocolate fan, you can omit them or swap them out with dark chocolate chips.

Yield: 24 small bars

CRUST

1 cup granulated sugar

2 cups all-purpose flour

⅔ cup old-fashioned oats

1 teaspoon baking powder

¼ teaspoon kosher salt

Zest of one orange

1 cup (2 sticks) unsalted butter, chilled

1 egg

½ cup white chocolate chips

FILLING

½ cup granulated sugar

4 teaspoons cornstarch

Juice of 1 orange

4 cups fresh raspberries

Crust

Preheat the oven to 375°F. Grease a 9 x 13-inch baking dish. Combine the sugar, flour, oats, baking powder, salt, and orange zest. Add the butter and the egg until the dough is crumbly. Fold in the white chocolate chips. Separate the mixture in half, pressing the first portion of the dough to the bottom of the baking dish.

Filling

In a separate bowl, combine the sugar, cornstarch, and orange juice. Gently fold in the raspberries until they are distributed evenly. Spread the raspberry mixture evenly across the first layer of dough. Crumble the remaining dough over the fruit. Bake for 30 to 40 minutes or until the crumble is golden brown. Allow to cool before cutting.

Cranberry Crumble

This wintery crumble is just the right set of flavors in the colder months. With fresh cranberries and a hint of rosemary herb, it's a truly festive treat.

Yield: 6–8 servings

FILLING

2 cups fresh cranberries

2 cups fresh raspberries

Juice of 1 orange

¾ cup granulated sugar

2 tablespoons flour

1 teaspoon rosemary, finely chopped

½ cup walnuts, chopped

¼ teaspoon kosher salt

TOPPING

1 cup Rice Krispies

½ cup flour

Zest of 1 orange

1 teaspoon rosemary, finely chopped

½ cup walnuts, chopped

½ teaspoon pumpkin pie spice

¼ teaspoon kosher salt

¼ cup butter, softened

Filling
Preheat the oven to 350°F. Grease an 8-inch baking dish. Add the cranberries and raspberries to the dish. Mix in the orange juice. Add the sugar, flour, rosemary, walnuts, and salt to the dish, and stir until the cranberries and raspberries are coated evenly. Place the dish in the oven for 15 minutes while preparing the topping.

Topping
In a separate bowl, combine the Rice Krispies, flour, orange zest, rosemary, walnuts, pumpkin pie spice, and salt. Cut in butter. Remove the baking dish from the oven. Sprinkle the topping evenly over the filling. Bake for another 15 to 20 minutes or until the crumble is golden brown and the juices are bubbling.

CHAPTER TWO

PEACHES, PLUMS, AND STONE FRUITS

Apricot Crumble Bars

Dried apricots are a prize to be savored, but this cobbler is an exceptional way to enjoy fresh apricots when they are in season. Finish the cobbler with whipped cream or our Vanilla Cream Sauce (page 114) for a truly indulgent experience.

Yield: 6–8 servings

CRUST

2 cups all-purpose flour

½ cup granulated sugar

¼ teaspoon kosher salt

1 cup (2 sticks) salted butter, chilled

FILLING

4 cups chopped apricots (about 12–15 whole)

⅔ cup sugar

1 tablespoon all-purpose flour

1 tablespoon fresh lemon juice

¾ teaspoon vanilla extract

TOPPING

½ cup butter, softened

½ cup granulated sugar

½ cup light brown sugar

½ cup all-purpose flour

1 teaspoon cinnamon

Crust

Preheat the oven to 350°F. Grease a 9 x 13-inch baking dish. Combine the flour, sugar, and salt. Slice the butter into pats and cut into the flour mixture with a pastry cutter or fork until crumbly. Press the mixture onto the base of the baking dish until you have made a smooth, even layer. Bake for 20 minutes.

Filling

Peel, pit, and slice the apricots. In the baking dish or a bowl, gently toss the apricots with the sugar, flour, lemon juice, and vanilla extract until the fruit is coated evenly. Remove crust from the oven. Layer the fruit filling over the crust and press down firmly.

Topping

In a separate bowl, make the streusel by creaming the butter, and then gradually adding the sugars until mixed. Gradually add the flour and cinnamon until blended. Sprinkle the top generously with the streusel. Return to the oven and bake for 15 to 20 minutes.

Peach Scone Cobbler

It sounds so simple, but warm peaches and fresh scones are nothing short of heavenly. This easy scone recipe takes the place of the usual biscuit dough; meanwhile, there are enough peaches in the dough and the filling to make sure that you never miss a bite of their fresh, sweet goodness.

Yield: 6–8 servings

FILLING

4 cups sliced peaches (about 4 whole)

¾ cup granulated sugar

1 tablespoon cornstarch

¼ cup fresh lemon juice

TOPPING

2 cups flour

1 tablespoon baking powder

¾ teaspoon salt

⅓ cup granulated sugar

4 tablespoons butter

2 tablespoons shortening

¾ cup cream

1 egg

1 cup diced peaches (about 1 whole)

Filling
Preheat the oven to 375°F. Grease an 8-inch baking dish. In the baking dish, gently toss the peaches with the sugar, cornstarch, and lemon juice until the fruit is coated evenly.

Topping
In a separate bowl, combine the flour, baking powder, salt, and sugar. Cut the butter and shortening into the flour mixture with a pastry cutter. In a separate bowl, combine the cream and egg until blended, then add to the dry ingredients. Fold in the peaches. On a lightly floured surface, roll out the dough and cut into biscuit rounds. Place the scones on top of the filling. Bake for 25 to 30 minutes or until the top is golden brown and the juices are bubbling.

Plum Cobbler

While peaches often get all the attention in the cobbler game, we've found that plums can sometimes steal the show. This delicious cobbler lets the soft and tart plums take the lead, resulting in a zesty cobbler that's not too sweet and not too juicy. If you want your biscuit topping to be a little closer to the sweeter side than buttery, just sift some confectioner's sugar over the crust once it has cooled down a bit from the oven.

Yield: 6–8 servings

FILLING

4 cups sliced plums (about 8 whole)

½ cup sugar

1 tablespoon cornstarch

1 tablespoon fresh lemon juice

TOPPING

1½ cups all-purpose flour

¼ cup granulated sugar

1½ teaspoons baking powder

¼ teaspoon kosher salt

1 teaspoon lemon zest

1½ tablespoons unsalted butter, chilled

1 cup buttermilk

Filling

Preheat the oven to 400°F. Grease an 8-inch baking dish. Pit and slice the plums, adding them to the pan. In the baking dish, gently toss the plums with the sugar, cornstarch, and lemon juice until they are coated evenly.

Topping

In a separate bowl, combine the flour, granulated sugar, baking powder, salt, and lemon zest. Slice the butter into pats and cut into the flour mixture with a pastry cutter or fork until crumbly. Add the buttermilk and fold into the dry ingredients until just combined. Drop the dough by rounded tablespoons onto the filling. Bake for 30 to 40 minutes or until the top is golden brown and the juices are bubbling.

Skillet Cherry-Berry Crisp

This cherry, raspberry, and strawberry crisp is as easy to prepare as it is pleasant to eat. You can warm the skillet in the oven as you are putting the rest of the ingredients together to help get you go from dessert-deprived to dessert-delighted in even less time.

Yield: 6–8 servings

FILLING

3 cups pitted cherries

1 cup raspberries

2 cups sliced strawberries

¼ cup sugar

¼ cup all-purpose flour

TOPPING

¾ cup all-purpose flour

½ cup brown sugar

2 tablespoons granulated sugar

¼ teaspoon nutmeg

½ teaspoon kosher salt

½ cup (1 stick) unsalted butter, room temperature

1 cup old-fashioned oats

Filling

Preheat the oven to 400°F. Grease a 12-inch skillet. In the skillet, gently toss the cherries, raspberries, and strawberries with the sugar and flour until the fruit is coated evenly.

Topping

In a separate bowl, combine the, flour, sugars, nutmeg, and salt. Slice the butter into pats and add to the mixture. Mix the butter and the dry ingredients, except the oats, until blended. Add the oats and knead the mixture until it becomes clumpy. Sprinkle the topping evenly over the filling. Bake for 30 to 40 minutes or until the top is golden brown and the juices are bubbling.

Nectarine & Raspberry Buckle

Buckle up, this lovely mix of sugary raspberries and nectarines makes this cousin of the cobbler nothing short of incredible. A little bit cakier than a cobbler or even a grunt, but with the right amount of fruit and cinnamon, this buckle is perfect, whether you're fancying some afternoon tea or just a late-night snack.

Yield: 24 small bars

FILLING

½ cup (1 stick) butter

¾ cup granulated sugar

2 eggs

1 teaspoon vanilla

2 cups all-purpose flour

2 teaspoons baking powder

½ teaspoon kosher salt

½ cup milk

1 cup fresh raspberries

2 cups pitted, chopped nectarines (about 3 whole)

TOPPING

⅓ cup all-purpose flour

⅓ cup brown sugar

1 teaspoon cinnamon

3 tablespoons butter, chilled

Filling

Preheat the oven to 350°F. Grease an 8-inch baking dish. In a separate bowl, combine the butter and sugar until creamy. Beat in the eggs one at a time, then add the vanilla. Combine the flour, baking powder, and salt. Gradually add in these dry ingredients and the milk until blended. Fold in the raspberries and nectarines. Scrape batter into prepared dish.

Topping

Combine the flour, brown sugar, and cinnamon. Slice the butter into pats and cut into the flour mixture with a pastry cutter or fork until crumbly. Sprinkle the topping evenly over the filling. Bake for 30 to 40 minutes or until the top is golden brown and the juices are bubbling.

Plum-Peach Crumble

In this recipe, two stone fruits work well together, with the subtle tartness of plums complementing the welcome comfort of warm peaches.

Yield: 6–8 servings

FILLING

½ cup granulated sugar

1 tablespoon cornstarch

¼ teaspoon ground cinnamon

¼ teaspoon ground ginger

¼ teaspoon ground cardamom

2 cups pitted, chopped plums (about 4 whole)

2 cups pitted, chopped peaches (about 3 medium)

¼ cup plum jam

TOPPING

¾ cup flour

3 tablespoons brown sugar

¼ teaspoon cinnamon

⅓ cup unsalted butter, room temperature

Filling

Preheat the oven to 375°F. Grease an 8-inch baking dish. Combine the sugar, cornstarch, cinnamon, ginger, and cardamom. In the baking dish, gently toss the mixture with the fruit until it is coated evenly. Stir in the jam.

Topping

In a separate bowl, combine the flour, brown sugar, and cinnamon. Slice the butter into pats and add to the mixture. Mix the butter and the dry ingredients with your hands until it forms small, crumbly pebbles. Sprinkle the crumble evenly over the top of the filling. Bake for 30 to 40 minutes or until the crumble is golden brown and the juices are bubbling.

Cocoa Plum & Nectarine Crisp

With just the right balance of tart and sweet, this plum and nectarine crisp is a dessert dazzler. The hint of cocoa powder is a nice touch for chocolate lovers.

Yield: 6–8 servings

FILLING

2 cups pitted, chopped plums (about 4 whole)

2 cups pitted, chopped nectarines (about 2 medium)

1 cup granulated sugar

1 tablespoon cornstarch

¼ teaspoon ground cinnamon

¼ teaspoon ground ginger

1 teaspoon cocoa powder

TOPPING

¾ cup all-purpose flour

½ cup brown sugar

2 tablespoons granulated sugar

½ teaspoon kosher salt

½ cup (1 stick) unsalted butter, room temperature

1 cup old-fashioned oats

Filling

Preheat the oven to 375°F. Grease an 8-inch baking dish. Pit and slice the plums and nectarines, adding them to the pan. Add the sugar, cornstarch, cinnamon, ginger, and cocoa powder to the dish and stir until the fruit is coated evenly.

Topping

In a separate bowl, combine the flour, sugars, and salt. Slice the butter into pats and add to the mixture. Mix the butter and the dry ingredients—except for the oats—until blended. Add the oats and knead the mixture until it becomes clumpy. Sprinkle the rest evenly over the top of the pears. Bake for 40 to 50 minutes or until the top is golden brown and the juices are bubbling.

Flaky Peach Cobbler

This flaky peach cobbler is the fraternal twin of a fresh-from-the-oven peach pie. It has the same buttery top crust, but skips the hassle of the bottom layer so that the peaches can really shine. The crust is simple to make, but if you're short on time, you can replace it with store-bought crust and focus your attention on the presentation of a dessert that's just peachy.

Yield: 6–8 servings

FILLING

6 cups pitted, sliced peaches (about 6 medium)

1 cup sugar

1 tablespoon cornstarch

1 tablespoon fresh lemon juice

TOPPING

1¼ cups all-purpose flour

½ teaspoon kosher salt

½ cup shortening

About 3 tablespoons ice water

4 tablespoons melted butter

1 tablespoon granulated sugar

1 teaspoon cinnamon

Filling

Preheat the oven to 375°. Grease a 9 x 13-inch baking dish. In the baking dish, gently toss the peaches with the sugar, cornstarch, and lemon juice until they are coated evenly.

Topping

In a separate bowl, combine the flour, salt, and shortening, mixing until crumbly. Add 2 tablespoons water and mix together, adding more water as needed to make a shaggy dough. On a lightly floured surface, knead the mixture for 2 to 3 minutes until it comes together. Cover and let chill for 30 minutes. On a lightly floured surface, roll out the dough and lay over the filling (dough can be cut into strips and arranged in a basket weave as well). Brush the topping with melted butter. Mix the sugar and cinnamon together and then sprinkle over the topping. Bake for 30 to 40 minutes or until the top is golden brown and the juices are bubbling.

Orange Liqueur-Cherry Clafoutis

A classic dessert paying homage to a classic cocktail, this cherry grunt is flavored with orange liqueur in the style of an Old Fashioned. The orange and cherry flavors were made for each other, making this a go-to combination. If you prefer not to use alcohol in this dessert, you can substitute orange juice, but the effect will be different.

Yield: 6–8 servings

FILLING

6 cups pitted, sliced cherries

¾ cup brown sugar

2 tablespoons all-purpose flour

½ cup orange liqueur (such as Grand Marnier or Cointreau)

TOPPING

2 large eggs

¾ cup granulated sugar

1 cup all-purpose flour

1 teaspoon baking powder

1 teaspoon kosher salt

1 cup whole milk

Filling

Preheat the oven to 350°F. Grease an 8-inch baking dish or ramekins. Stir the cherries, brown sugar, flour, and orange liqueur together until the fruit is coated evenly.

Topping

Whip together eggs and sugar until light and fluffy. Stir in the flour, baking powder, salt, and milk until just combined. Pour the batter over the filling. Bake for 30 minutes or until the top is golden brown and the juices are bubbling.

Peach & Orange Shortcake Cobbler

Buttery shortbread makes this peach cobbler taste like home. With a little taste of orange coming in behind the peach, this dessert has just the right balance of citrus and zest. You can also add a little bit of cinnamon to the fruit filling for a bit more spice.

Yield: 6–8 servings

FILLING

4 cups pitted, sliced peaches (about 4 medium)

½ cup sugar

1 tablespoon cornstarch

Juice of 1 orange

TOPPING

1½ cups all-purpose flour

¼ cup granulated sugar

1½ teaspoons baking powder

¼ teaspoon kosher salt

Zest of 1 orange

1½ tablespoons unsalted butter, chilled

¾ cup buttermilk

Filling

Preheat the oven to 400°F. Grease an 8-inch baking dish. In the baking dish, gently toss the peaches with the sugar, cornstarch, and orange juice until the fruit is coated evenly.

Topping

In a separate bowl, combine the flour, granulated sugar, baking powder, salt, and orange zest. Slice the butter into pats and cut into the flour mixture with a pastry cutter or fork until crumbly. Add the buttermilk and fold into the dry ingredients until just combined. Drop the dough by rounded tablespoons onto the filling. Bake for 30 to 40 minutes or until the top is golden brown and the juices are bubbling.

Plum Upside-Down Crisp

Take your crisp and cobbler game to the next level with these crunchy plum bars. They have all the same crispy goodness as a traditional crisp but in a slightly tidier package, and are a great way to take advantage of delicious seasonal plums.

Yield: 24 small bars

CRUST

1 cup granulated sugar

1 cup old-fashioned oats

2 cups all-purpose flour

1 teaspoon baking powder

½ teaspoon salt

1 teaspoon lemon zest

1 cup (2 sticks) unsalted butter, chilled

1 egg

FILLING

½ cup granulated sugar

1 tablespoon cornstarch

2 tablespoons fresh lemon juice

4 cups pitted, sliced plums (about 8 whole)

Crust

Preheat the oven to 375°F. Grease a 9 x 13-inch baking dish. Combine the sugar, oats, flour, baking powder, salt, and lemon zest. Add the butter and the egg until the dough is crumbly. Separate the mixture in half, pressing the first part of the dough into the bottom of the baking dish.

Filling

In a large bowl, combine the sugar, cornstarch, and lemon juice. Fold in the plums. Spread the plum mixture evenly across the first layer of dough. Crumble the remaining dough over the fruit. Bake for 30 to 40 minutes or until the crumble is golden brown.

CHAPTER THREE

APPLES, PEARS, AND ORCHARD FRUITS

Apple-Gingersnap Crumble

Gingersnaps have found their rightful home atop this incredible cobbler. The spicy ginger is the perfect complement to the apples, making for a comforting fall favorite.

Yield: 6–8 servings

FILLING

4 cups sliced apples (about 4 medium)

2 tablespoons fresh lemon juice

½ teaspoon vanilla

¼ teaspoon cinnamon

½ cup brown sugar

2 tablespoons cornstarch

¼ teaspoon kosher salt

TOPPING

2 cups gingersnaps, crushed

1½ cups all-purpose flour

¼ teaspoon kosher salt

½ cup (1 stick) unsalted butter

Filling

Preheat the oven to 375°F. Grease an 8-inch baking dish. In the baking dish, toss the apples with the lemon juice. Add the vanilla, cinnamon, brown sugar, cornstarch, and salt to the dish and stir until the apples are coated evenly.

Topping

In a separate bowl, combine the crushed gingersnaps, flour, and salt. Slice the butter into pats and add to the mixture. Mix the butter and the dry ingredients with your hands until it forms small, crumbly pebbles. Add half of the mixture to the baking dish, stirring into the apple filling evenly. Sprinkle the rest evenly over the top of the apples. Bake for 30 to 40 minutes or until the crumble is golden brown and the juices are bubbling.

Apple-Blackberry Crisp

This crunchy dessert marries the tartness of the blackberries with the subtle sweetness of the apples for a match made in heaven.

Yield: 6–8 servings

FILLING

½ cup brown sugar

2 tablespoons fresh lemon juice

2 tablespoons cornstarch

3 cups chopped apples (about 4 medium)

1 cup blackberries

TOPPING

¾ cup all-purpose flour

½ cup brown sugar

½ teaspoon kosher salt

¼ teaspoon ground cinnamon

¼ teaspoon ground ginger

½ cup (1 stick) unsalted butter

1 cup old-fashioned oats

Filling

Preheat the oven to 375°F. Grease an 8-inch baking dish. Stir the brown sugar, lemon juice, and cornstarch with the apples until the apples are coated evenly. Over medium heat, cook the apples until they are tender, about 5 minutes. Transfer the apples to the baking dish, and then arrange the blackberries on top.

Topping

In a separate bowl, combine the flour, brown sugar, salt, cinnamon, and ginger. Slice the butter into pats and add to the mixture. Mix the butter and the dry ingredients—except the oats—until blended. Add the oats and knead the mixture until it becomes clumpy. Sprinkle the topping evenly over the filling. Bake for 40 to 50 minutes or until the top is golden brown and the juices are bubbling.

Apple-Peach Crumble

Now the choice between warm apple crisp and homey peach cobbler is moot. Try drizzling our incredible Bourbon Caramel Sauce (page 110) over this tasty dessert for even more flavor power.

Yield: 6–8 servings

FILLING

2 cups sliced apples (about 2 medium)

2 cups pitted, sliced peaches (about 2 medium)

2 tablespoons fresh lemon juice

½ teaspoon vanilla

¾ cup sugar

½ teaspoon cinnamon

2 tablespoons cornstarch

¼ teaspoon kosher salt

TOPPING

1½ cups all-purpose flour

1 cup brown sugar

½ teaspoon cinnamon

¼ teaspoon freshly grated nutmeg

¼ teaspoon kosher salt

½ cup (1 stick) unsalted butter, room temperature

Filling

Preheat the oven to 375°F. Grease an 8-inch baking dish. In the baking dish, toss the apples and peaches with the lemon juice. Add the vanilla, sugar, cinnamon, cornstarch, and salt to the dish and stir until the apples are coated evenly.

Topping

In a separate bowl, combine the flour, brown sugar, cinnamon, nutmeg, and salt. Slice the butter into pats and add to the mixture. Mix the butter and the dry ingredients with your hands until it forms small, crumbly pebbles. Add half of the mixture to the baking dish, stirring into the fruit filling evenly. Sprinkle the rest evenly over the top of the filling. Bake for 30 to 40 minutes or until the crumble is golden brown and the juices are bubbling.

Apple-Cherry Crumble

An apple crisp is so delicious on its own that it seems unnecessary to fancy it up with other ingredients, but the cherries here are no mistake. With a little bit of vanilla in the mix to bring the fruit flavors together, this crumble is sure to be a new favorite.

Yield: 6–8 servings

FILLING

2 cups chopped apples (about 2 medium)

2 cups pitted cherries

2 tablespoons fresh lemon juice

½ teaspoon vanilla

¾ cup brown sugar

½ teaspoon cinnamon

2 tablespoons cornstarch

¼ teaspoon kosher salt

TOPPING

1½ cups all-purpose flour

1 cup brown sugar

½ teaspoon cinnamon

¼ teaspoon freshly grated nutmeg

¼ teaspoon kosher salt

½ cup (1 stick) unsalted butter, room temperature

Filling

Preheat the oven to 375°F. Grease an 8-inch baking dish. In the baking dish toss the apples and cherries with the lemon juice. Add the vanilla, brown sugar, cinnamon, cornstarch, and salt to the dish and stir until the fruit is coated evenly.

Topping

In a separate bowl, combine the flour, brown sugar, cinnamon, nutmeg, and salt. Slice the butter into pats and add to the mixture. Mix the butter and the dry ingredients with your hands until it forms small, crumbly pebbles. Add half of the mixture to the baking dish, stirring into the fruit filling evenly. Sprinkle the rest evenly over the top of the filling. Bake for 30 to 40 minutes or until the crumble is golden brown and the juices are bubbling.

Ginger-Pear Crisp

With spicy ginger and mild pears, this dessert has two flavor profiles that are just right together. Top it with Almond Whipped Cream (page 111) for even more depth to this decadent dessert.

Yield: 6–8 servings

FILLING

4 cups chopped pears (about 4 medium)

1 tablespoon fresh lemon juice

1½ tablespoons all-purpose flour

½ cup granulated sugar

1 tablespoon ginger

TOPPING

¾ cup all-purpose flour

½ cup brown sugar

2 tablespoons granulated sugar

½ teaspoon kosher salt

½ cup (1 stick) unsalted butter, room temperature

1 cup old-fashioned oats

Filling

Preheat the oven to 375°F. Grease an 8-inch baking dish. In the baking dish, toss the pears with the lemon juice. Add the flour, sugar, and ginger to the dish and stir until the pears are coated evenly.

Topping

In a separate bowl, combine the flour, sugars, and salt. Slice the butter into pats and add to the mixture. Mix the butter and the dry ingredients, except the oats, until blended. Add the oats and knead the mixture until it becomes clumpy. Sprinkle the rest evenly over the top of the pears. Bake for 40 to 50 minutes or until the top is golden brown and the juices are bubbling.

Chocolate-Pear Crisp

Chocoholics, rejoice! While crisps, crumbles, and cobblers rarely get to feature chocolate in the mix, this combination is a winner. Feel free to adjust the amount of chocolate chips that best works for your sweet tooth.

Yield: 6–8 servings

FILLING

4 cups chopped pears (about 6 medium)

1 tablespoon fresh lemon juice

1½ tablespoons all-purpose flour

½ cup granulated sugar

1 teaspoon ginger

TOPPING

¾ cup all-purpose flour

½ cup brown sugar

2 tablespoons granulated sugar

½ teaspoon kosher salt

½ cup (1 stick) unsalted butter, room temperature

1 cup old-fashioned oats

½ cup semi-sweet chocolate chips

Filling

Preheat the oven to 375°F. Grease an 8-inch baking dish. In the baking dish, toss the pears with the lemon juice. Add the flour, sugar, and ginger to the dish and stir until the pears are coated evenly.

Topping

In a separate bowl, combine the flour, sugars, and salt. Slice the butter into pats and add to the mixture. Mix the butter and the dry ingredients, except the oats and chocolate chips, until blended. Add the oats and chocolate chips, and then knead the mixture until it becomes clumpy. Sprinkle the rest evenly over the top of the pears. Bake for 40 to 50 minutes or until the top is golden brown and the juices are bubbling.

Old-Fashioned Apple-Pear Grunt

This cakey, flaky grunt is a taste of home. The subtle pairing of apples and pears makes for a comforting and sweet dessert. When you've poured the topping over the fruit, dress up the presentation by lining even slices of apples or pears along the top.

Yield: 6–8 servings

FILLING

1 cup granulated sugar

1 tablespoon cornstarch

1 teaspoon vanilla

½ teaspoon cinnamon

¼ teaspoon kosher salt

2 cups sliced apples (about 2 medium)

2 cups sliced pears (about 2 medium)

TOPPING

1 cup all-purpose flour

¾ cup granulated sugar

1 teaspoon baking powder

1 teaspoon kosher salt

1 large egg

1 cup whole milk

Filling

Preheat the oven to 350°F. Grease an 8-inch baking dish. Combine the sugar, cornstarch, vanilla, cinnamon, and salt. Gently toss with the fruit in the baking dish until it is coated evenly.

Topping

In a separate bowl, combine the flour, sugar, baking powder, and salt. Whisk in the egg and milk until combined. Pour the batter over the filling. Bake for 30 minutes or until the top is golden brown and the juices are bubbling.

Apple-Raisin Grunt

There's no need to visit an apple orchard for the taste of fall that this exquisite dessert offers. The raisins add just the right amount of sweetness and texture to the mix, while the subtly spiced, cakey grunt topping blankets the apples for a cozy, delectable seasonal treat.

Yield: 6–8 servings

FILLING

2 cups chopped apples (about 2 medium)

¾ cup raisins

½ cup granulated sugar

TOPPING

1 cup all-purpose flour

1 cup granulated sugar

1 teaspoon baking powder

½ teaspoon pumpkin pie spice

½ teaspoon kosher salt

2 teaspoons lemon zest

1 cup milk

2 tablespoons fresh lemon juice

1 teaspoon vanilla

Filling

Preheat the oven to 375°F. Heavily grease a 10-inch cast-iron skillet and let it warm in the oven. Toss the apples with the raisins and sugar, then set them aside.

Topping

In a separate bowl, combine the flour, sugar, baking powder, pumpkin pie spice, salt, and lemon zest. Whisk in the milk, lemon juice, and vanilla until combined. Carefully remove the skillet from the oven and add the apple-raisin mixture. Pour the batter over the filling. Return the skillet to the oven and bake for 30 minutes or until the top is golden brown and the juices are bubbling.

Pecan-Apple Cinnamon Betty

Apple betties are a classic for a reason, but the added pecans put this dessert over the top. With a nice crunch and a bit of cinnamon to bring out the flavors of the apples, this betty is a comforting way to end any meal.

Yield: 6–8 servings

FILLING

4 cups sliced apples (about 4 medium)

2 tablespoons fresh lemon juice

½ teaspoon vanilla

½ cup granulated sugar

¼ cup brown sugar

½ teaspoon cinnamon

2 tablespoons cornstarch

¼ teaspoon kosher salt

TOPPING

1½ cups all-purpose flour

1 cup brown sugar

½ teaspoon cinnamon

¼ teaspoon freshly grated nutmeg

¼ teaspoon kosher salt

½ cup (1 stick) unsalted butter, room temperature

½ cup pecans

Filling

Preheat the oven to 375°F. Grease an 8-inch baking dish. In the baking dish, toss the apples with the lemon juice. Add the vanilla, sugars, cinnamon, cornstarch, and salt to the dish and stir until the apples are coated evenly.

Topping

In a separate bowl, combine the flour, brown sugar, cinnamon, nutmeg, and salt. Slice the butter into pats and add to the mixture. Mix the butter and the dry ingredients with your hands until it forms small, crumbly pebbles. Mix in the nuts. Sprinkle the topping evenly over the top of the apples. Bake for 30 to 40 minutes or until the crumble is golden brown and the juices are bubbling.

Apple Pie Bars

There's no marshmallow fluff here, but these treats combine the satisfying texture of crispy rice with the sweetness of apples.

Yield: 24 small bars

FILLING

6 tablespoons butter

¾ cup granulated sugar

2 eggs

1 teaspoon vanilla

2 cups all-purpose flour

2 teaspoons baking powder

½ teaspoon kosher salt

½ cup milk

2 cups chopped apples (about 2 whole)

TOPPING

⅓ cup all-purpose flour

¼ cup brown sugar

1 teaspoon cinnamon

3 tablespoons butter, chilled

½ cup Rice Krispies

Filling

Preheat the oven to 350°F. Grease an 8-inch baking dish. In a separate bowl, combine the butter and sugar until creamy. Beat in the eggs one at a time, then add the vanilla. Combine the flour, baking powder, and salt. Gradually add in these dry ingredients and the milk until blended. Fold in the apples and add the batter to the dish.

Topping

Combine the flour, brown sugar, and cinnamon. Slice the butter into pats and cut into the flour mixture with a pastry cutter or fork until crumbly. Gently fold in the Rice Krispies. Sprinkle the topping evenly over the filling. Bake for 30 to 40 minutes or until the top is golden brown and the juices are bubbling.

Apple-Walnut Streusel

The only thing better than traditional cinnamon streusel is one with a little extra crunch. This apple crisp switches it up a bit, with walnuts adding far more crunch than a typical crisp with oats. Depending on your preference, you can leave the walnuts whole or chop them to play with the texture.

Yield: 6–8 servings

FILLING

4 cups sliced apples (about 4 medium)

2 tablespoons fresh lemon juice

½ teaspoon vanilla

½ cup brown sugar

½ teaspoon cinnamon

3 tablespoons cornstarch

¼ teaspoon kosher salt

TOPPING

1½ cups all-purpose flour

1 cup brown sugar

½ teaspoon cinnamon

¼ teaspoon freshly grated nutmeg

¼ teaspoon kosher salt

½ cup (1 stick) unsalted butter, room temperature

¼ cup walnuts

Filling

Preheat the oven to 375°F. Grease an 8-inch baking dish. In the baking dish, toss the apples with the lemon juice. Add the vanilla, brown sugar, cinnamon, cornstarch, and salt to the dish and stir until the apples are coated evenly.

Topping

In a separate bowl, combine the flour, brown sugar, cinnamon, nutmeg, and salt. Slice the butter into pats and add to the mixture. Mix the butter and the dry ingredients with your hands until it forms small, crumbly pebbles. Mix in the nuts. Sprinkle the topping evenly over the top of the apples. Bake for 30 to 40 minutes or until the crumble is golden brown and the juices are bubbling.

CHAPTER FOUR

PUMPKIN, PINEAPPLE, AND MORE

Pumpkin Cheesecake Crumble

No need for pumpkin spice lattes when you have this delicious pumpkin cheesecake crumble. This recipe doesn't include a gingerbread crust as seen in a typical cheesecake, but with this tasty crisp, you won't even miss it. Serve layered with whipped cream in parfait glasses for a special treat.

Yield: 6–8 servings

FILLING

2 (8-ounce) packages cream cheese, softened

1 (15-ounce) can of pumpkin purée

2 eggs

1 teaspoon cinnamon

1 cup granulated sugar

TOPPING

½ cup old-fashioned oats

½ cup graham crackers, crushed

½ cup (1 stick) unsalted butter, chilled

Filling

Preheat the oven to 400°F. Grease an 8-inch baking dish. Beat the cream cheese until smooth, and then mix in the pumpkin purée. Add the eggs and beat the mixture until combined. Mix in the cinnamon and sugar, then pour into the dish.

Topping

In a separate bowl, toss the oats and the crushed graham crackers together. Slice the butter into pats and cut into the dry mixture with a pastry cutter or fork until crumbly. Sprinkle the blend on top of the filling. Bake for 25 minutes or until the top is golden brown.

Lemon Squares

Lemons just don't jive with a typical recipe for a cobbler or crisp, but it would be a shame to skip over them entirely. Simple lemon squares are well-loved by many, and this recipe offers all of the delicious citrusy lemon goodness and sweet powdered sugar that make this recipe easy and an all-time favorite.

Yield: 6–8 servings

CRUST

2 cups all-purpose flour

½ cup granulated sugar

¼ teaspoon kosher salt

1 cup (2 sticks) salted butter, chilled

TOPPING

¼ cup flour

1½ cups granulated sugar

4 eggs

½ cup fresh lemon juice (about 4 lemons)

2 teaspoons lemon zest

½ cup powdered sugar, or enough for sifting

Crust

Preheat the oven to 350°F. Grease an 8-inch baking dish. Combine the flour, sugar, and salt. Slice the butter into pats and cut into the flour mixture with a pastry cutter or fork until crumbly. Press the mixture onto the base of the baking dish until you have made a smooth, even layer. Bake for 20 minutes.

Topping

In a separate bowl, toss the flour and sugar together. Whisk in the eggs and then add the lemon juice and zest. Remove crust from the oven after 20 minutes are up. Pour the lemon mixture over the crust. Return to the oven and bake for another 20 minutes. Chill for at least 2 hours and sprinkle powdered sugar before cutting.

Papaya-Strawberry Cobbler

This spectacular cobbler just tastes like a tropical vacation. Papaya can be harder to find in stores depending on where you live, but it's well worth the hunt. The combination of the tropical fruit and sweet strawberries is an incredible blend of flavors and a nice balance of textures.

Yield: 6–8 servings

FILLING

2 cups peeled, seeded, sliced papaya (about 1 medium)

2 cups hulled, sliced strawberries

⅔ cup granulated sugar

1 tablespoon cornstarch

1 tablespoon fresh lemon juice

TOPPING

1½ cups all-purpose flour

¼ cup granulated sugar

1½ teaspoons baking powder

¼ teaspoon kosher salt

1 teaspoon lemon zest

1½ tablespoons unsalted butter, chilled

¾ cup buttermilk

Filling

Preheat the oven to 400°F. Grease an 8-inch baking dish. In the baking dish or a bowl, gently toss the papaya and strawberries with the sugar, cornstarch, and lemon juice until the fruit is coated evenly.

Topping

In a separate bowl, combine the flour, granulated sugar, baking powder, salt, and lemon zest. Slice the butter into pats and cut into the flour mixture with a pastry cutter or fork until crumbly. Add the buttermilk and fold into the dry ingredients until just combined. Drop the dough by rounded tablespoons onto the filling. Bake for 30 to 40 minutes or until the top is golden brown and the juices are bubbling.

Piña Colada Shortbread Crumble

If you can't make it to the tropics to sip on a frozen piña colada, this crumble may be an even better alternative. With a good helping of sweet, shredded coconut and juicy pineapples, this dessert will transport you to the sandy beaches you're looking for.

Yield: 6–8 servings

FILLING

3 (10-ounce) cans pineapple chunks, drained

3 tablespoons flour

½ cup brown sugar

TOPPING

1 cup (2 sticks) unsalted butter, room temperature

¾ cup granulated sugar

¼ teaspoon kosher salt

1½ teaspoons vanilla extract

1 egg yolk

2 cups all-purpose flour

1 cup sweetened shredded coconut, toasted

Filling

Preheat the oven to 375°F. Grease a 9 x 13-inch baking dish. Toss the pineapple with the flour and brown sugar until the fruit is coated evenly.

Topping

In a separate bowl, combine the butter, sugar, salt, and vanilla until smooth. Mix in the egg. Gradually add in the flour and mix until combined. Fold in the coconut. Separate the mixture in half and press the first portion to the bottom of the pan. Add the filling, and then press the remaining shortbread dough evenly over the top of the fruit mixture. Bake for 25 minutes or until the crumble is golden brown and the juices are bubbling.

Pumpkin Spice Crumble

Pumpkin is the gold standard of seasonal flavors, and this blend of spices and pumpkin purée makes this the quintessential fall dessert. The topping has its own dose of cinnamon added to it, so every bite—from the pumpkin-packed filling to the crispy crust—has the taste of fall.

Yield: 6–8 servings

FILLING

1 (15-ounce) can pumpkin purée

1 cup evaporated milk

2 eggs, beaten

½ cup granulated sugar

¼ cup brown sugar

1½ teaspoons pumpkin pie spice

½ teaspoon salt

TOPPING

¾ cup flour

3 tablespoons brown sugar

¼ teaspoon cinnamon

⅓ cup unsalted butter, room temperature

Filling
Preheat the oven to 350°F. Grease an 8-inch baking dish. Combine the pumpkin, evaporated milk, and eggs until blended. Gradually mix in the sugars, pumpkin pie spice, and salt until smooth. Pour the filling into the dish.

Topping

In a separate bowl, combine the flour, brown sugar, and cinnamon. Slice the butter into pats and add to the mixture. Mix the butter and the dry ingredients with your hands until it forms small, crumbly pebbles. Sprinkle the crumble evenly over the top of the filling. Bake for 30 to 40 minutes or until the crumble is golden brown and the juices are bubbling.

Pineapple-Mango Crumble

Macadamia nuts, shredded coconut, pineapple, and mango—this blend of flavors is as tropical as it gets. The nuts add just the right amount of texture to balance out the sweet fruits. While pineapple takes center stage in this recipe, feel free to swap the proportions if you favor mangoes.

Yield: 6–8 servings

FILLING

¾ cup granulated sugar

2 tablespoons flour

2 tablespoons instant tapioca

¼ teaspoon kosher salt

3 (10-ounce) cans pineapple chunks, drained

2 cups peeled, sliced mango (about 1 medium)

TOPPING

1¼ cups all-purpose flour

¾ cup macadamia nuts, chopped

⅓ cup sweetened shredded coconut, toasted

½ cup (1 stick) unsalted butter, chilled

Filling

Preheat the oven to 375°F. Grease a 9 x 13-inch baking dish. Combine the sugar, flour, tapioca, and salt, and then gently toss with the fruit until the pineapple and mango are coated evenly.

Topping

In a separate bowl, combine the flour, macadamia nuts, and coconut. Slice the butter into pats and cut into the flour mixture with a pastry cutter or fork until crumbly. Reserve a bit of the mixture, but press most of it into the bottom of the pan. Add the filling, and then crumble the rest of the mixture evenly over the filling. Bake for 30 to 40 minutes or until the crumble is golden brown and the juices are bubbling.

Nutty Bananas Foster Crumble

Bananas foster is one of those desserts that seems to have endless iterations—from a simple topping to the focus of pancakes or waffles. And it's just too good to not have a version in crumble form. This recipe sticks to its roots with incredible caramelized bananas and a satisfying crunch from the pecans.

Yield: 6–8 servings

FILLING

4 to 6 ripe bananas

½ cup (1 stick) unsalted butter, melted

3 tablespoons brown sugar

¼ cup bourbon, if desired

TOPPING

1 cup all-purpose flour

½ cup brown sugar

4 tablespoons (½ stick) unsalted butter, chilled

1 cup pecans, chopped

Filling

Preheat the oven to 350°F. Grease an 8-inch baking dish. Peel and slice the bananas, adding them to the dish. Drizzle the melted butter over the bananas. Stir in the brown sugar and the bourbon until the bananas are coated evenly.

Topping

In a separate bowl, combine the flour and brown sugar. Slice the butter into pats and cut into the mixture with a pastry cutter or fork until crumbly. Fold in the pecans until mixed. Sprinkle the topping evenly over the filling. Bake for 25 minutes or until the crumble is golden brown and the juices are bubbling.

Orange-Apricot & Coconut Crisp Bar

These bars are packed with flavor. With a whirl of pineapple, coconut, orange, and apricot (plus the crunch of macadamia nuts), the flavors just keep on coming in this fun, tasty take on a traditional crisp.

Yield: 24 small bars

FILLING

1 cup dried apricots

Juice and zest of 4 oranges

¼ cup brown sugar

1 cup crushed pineapple

CRUST

1 (18-ounce) box yellow cake mix

⅔ cup coconut milk

2 eggs

TOPPING

1 cup old-fashioned oats

1 cup macadamia nuts

¼ teaspoon ginger

½ teaspoon brown sugar

Filling

Preheat the oven to 350°F. Grease a 9 x 13-inch baking dish. In a small sauce-pan, cook the apricots, orange juice, orange zest, and brown sugar over medium-low heat. Stir in the pineapple and let simmer for another 5 minutes.

Remove the fruit filling from the heat and set aside to cool. Purée the mixture once it is no longer hot.

Crust

Combine the cake mix, coconut milk, and eggs until smooth but sticky. Reserve 1 cup of the cake mix and spread the rest out evenly on the bottom of the baking dish.

Topping

In a separate bowl, combine 1 cup cake batter, oats, macadamia nuts, ginger, and brown sugar. Spread the puréed fruit filling over the cake layer, and then crumble the oat and nut layer on top. Bake for 30 to 40 minutes or until the top is golden brown.

Mango-Ginger Crumble Bar

Mango and ginger is an unlikely pair that does not disappoint. This dessert is a no-fuss one, with a filling that lets the mango shine and a crumble topping that has a hint of ginger for an extra layer of incredible flavor.

Yield: 24 small bars

CRUST

1 cup granulated sugar

3 cups all-purpose flour

1 teaspoon baking powder

1 teaspoon ginger

¼ teaspoon salt

1 cup (2 sticks) unsalted butter, chilled

1 egg

FILLING

½ cup granulated sugar

4 teaspoons cornstarch

4 cups peeled, sliced mango (about 2 medium)

Crust

Preheat the oven to 375°F. Grease a 9 x 13-inch baking dish. Combine the sugar, flour, baking powder, ginger, and salt. Add the butter and the egg until the dough is crumbly. Separate the mixture in half, pressing half the dough to the bottom of the baking dish.

Filling

In a separate bowl, combine the sugar and cornstarch. Fold in the mango until combined thoroughly. Spread the mango mixture evenly across the first layer of dough. Crumble the remaining dough over the fruit. Bake for 30 to 40 minutes or until the crumble is golden brown. Allow to cool before cutting.

Lime-Coconut Crumble Bar

Lime in the coconut! A flavor combination worthy of its own song, these delicious bars are show-stopping. This dessert will gladden coconut enthusiasts (but don't eat so many that you get a belly ache).

Yield: 24 small bars

CRUST

1 cup brown sugar

2 cups all-purpose flour

1 teaspoon baking powder

¼ teaspoon salt

½ cup (1 stick) unsalted butter

1 egg

½ cup sweetened shredded coconut, plus more for sprinkling

½ cup old-fashioned oats

FILLING

1 (14-ounce) can sweetened condensed milk

Juice of 4 limes (about ½ cup)

Zest of one lime

½ teaspoon vanilla

Crust

Preheat the oven to 350°F. Grease an 8-inch baking dish. Combine the brown sugar, flour, baking powder, and salt. Add the butter and the egg until the dough is crumbly. Fold in the coconut and oats. Separate the mixture in half, pressing the first portion of the dough to the bottom of the baking dish.

Filling

In a separate bowl, combine the condensed milk, lime juice, lime zest, and vanilla. Pour the lime mixture evenly across the first layer of dough. Crumble the remaining dough over the lime layer. Bake for 30 to 40 minutes or until the crumble is golden brown. Sprinkle additional shredded coconut over the top. Allow to cool before cutting.

CHAPTER FIVE

SAUCES

Bourbon Caramel Sauce

Caramel sauce has no greater use than topping a delicious, crispy fruit dessert. Try this simple recipe with a hint of bourbon to help ramp up any of the recipes in this book. Buying caramel sauce might be easy, but so is making this!

Yield: About 2½ cups

1 cup brown sugar

½ cup half-and-half

¼ cup butter

⅛ teaspoon salt

1 tablespoon bourbon

½ teaspoon vanilla extract

Heat the brown sugar, half-and-half, butter, and salt in a saucepan over medium-low heat. Stir constantly until the sugar dissolves and the sauce has thickened, about 5 minutes. Add the bourbon and vanilla and let simmer for another minute. Remove from the heat and let cool before storing.

Almond Whipped Cream

This whipped cream is a subtle way to improve any fruit cobbler or crisp. With the cold and creamy taste of homemade whipped cream and a little hint of almond, you'll have a hard time not just eating it straight from the bowl.

Yield: About 2 cups

1 cup cold heavy cream

1 teaspoon almond extract or syrup

2 tablespoons sugar

In a large mixing bowl, stir the heavy cream and almond extract together until blended. Add the sugar and whip the mixture with a whisk or mixer until it holds stiff peaks.

Cappuccino Whipped Cream

Whipped cream is a natural with any hot fruit dessert, but this one is particularly divine. Use this to top the Chocolate-Pear Crisp (page 74), or even the fruit cobblers for a fun take on a delicious whipped topping. If you don't have espresso, you can use instant coffee as a substitute.

Yield: About 2 cups

1 cup cold heavy cream

1 teaspoon instant espresso powder

1 teaspoon vanilla

2 tablespoons sugar

In a large mixing bowl, stir the heavy cream, espresso powder, and vanilla together until blended. Add the sugar and whip the mixture with a whisk or mixer until it holds stiff peaks.

Vanilla Cream Sauce

Vanilla sauce goes with just about any of these desserts, especially the Tri-Berry Crumble (page 16) or the Apple-Gingersnap Crumble (page 64). This vanilla cream topping is easy to whip up, and will make the steaming hot fruit shine.

Yield: About 2 cups

1 cup granulated sugar

½ cup butter, softened

½ cup light cream

1 teaspoon vanilla extract

In a large mixing bowl, cut the sugar and butter together until blended. Add the cream and vanilla extract and whip the mixture until thoroughly mixed. Serve hot.

Cinnamon Sugar Glaze

Cinnamon buns shouldn't have all the fun. With only a few ingredients, it's easy to make a sticky, sugary glaze to drizzle on about any crumbly fruit recipe.

Yield: About 1 cup

1 cup confectionary sugar

2 tablespoons milk

½ teaspoon cinnamon

In a large mixing bowl, whisk the confectionary sugar, milk, and cinnamon together until well blended. To thicken, simply add more sugar until you reach the desired consistency.

Index